# The Big One

Susannah York was born in London and raised in Scotland. Study at the Royal Academy of Dramatic Art brought the Ronson Award as most promising student and marriage to Michael Wells. She has since starred in a wide variety of films, received an Oscar nomination for her Alice Leblanc in *They Shoot Horses Don't They?* and the Cannes Film Festival prize for Best Actress for her role in Robert Altman's *Images*. At least half her working life has been devoted to the theatre and she has played leading roles in London, New York and Paris. She is the author of two books, *In Search of Unicorns* and *Lark's Castle* (Hodder and Stoughton).

She lives south of the River Thames with her children Sacha and Orlando and various animals.

Bill Bachle is an American who arrived in Devon via Missouri, El Salvador, Peru, Switzerland, New York and San Francisco. He has written advertising, worked in rural health, coached basketball, written for Robert Kennedy and George McGovern, planted trees along the M5, created the Gun Control advertising campaign, and advised Peace Groups on communications. He is on the Co-ordinating Committee of END (European Nuclear Disarmament) and writes advertising for CND (Campaign for Nuclear Disarmament).

He is married, has four sons and tends a small-holding on the edge of Dartmoor.

*For Sasha, Matthew, Joe,*
*Orlando, Ben, Bobby*
*and all children everywhere*

When I grow up
I want to be
ALIVE..

# THE BIG ONE

*An anthology of original sketches,*
*poems, cartoons and songs on the theme of peace*

Edited by
Susannah York and Bill Bachle

METHUEN

A METHUEN PAPERBACK

First published in Great Britain in 1984
by Methuen London Ltd
11 New Fetter Lane, London EC4P 4EE

Howard Barker: Judy Daish Associates, 83 Eastbourne Mews,
London W2 6LQ
Alan Bleasdale: Harvey Unna and Steven Durbridge Ltd, 24 Pottery Lane,
London W11
Elvis Costello: Plangent Vision Music Ltd, 27 Noel St, London W1
Ian Dury: Warner Brothers Music Ltd, 17 Berners Street, London W1
David Hare: Margaret Ramsay Ltd, 14A Goodwin's Court,
St Martin's Lane, London WC2 4LL
Terry Johnson: Goodwin Associates, 19 London St, London W2
Stephen Lowe: Margaret Ramsay Ltd, 14A Goodwin's Court,
St Martin's Lane, London WC2 4LL
Andrew Marshall and David Renwick: Sheila Lemon Ltd, Assets House,
17 Elverton St, London SW1
Anthony Matheson: London Management & Representation Ltd,
235 Regent St, London W1
Adrian Mitchell: Fraser and Dunlop (Scripts) Ltd, 91 Regent St,
London W1
Harold Pinter: ACTAC Ltd, 16 Cadogan Lane, London SW1
Emma Thompson: Noel Gay Artists Ltd, 24 Denmark Street,
London WC2H 8NJ

Made and printed in Great Britain

ISBN 0 413 55910 6

# Contents

The colour drawings between pages 42 and 43 are
by Gerald Scarfe

# Introduction

How did this book come to be?

Last year on 18 December we staged a show at the Apollo Victoria in London in which the people in this book and many others – writers, musicians, artists, and technicians – gave generously of their time and talents to look at the nuclear issue in their own ways: ways that were startling, outrageous, desperate, and often very funny. They gave because like people everywhere, they view the increased armed nature of our world with increasing alarm.

Clemenceau wrote: 'Governments' most important task is to make Peace more exciting than War by encouraging the Arts.' The mounting expenditure by our government on Britain's nuclear weapons at huge cost to our educational and social services, with all their inbuilt risks of accident, has made us yearn for a quality of life we know of; whilst the deployment of cruise missiles on our soil has made many 'middle of the road' people realise that Britain herself is in the middle of a nuclear battlefield. Far more powerful however, we believe, than the military hardware – than these machines created out of fear – can be the forces arrayed against them: the will for survival and the irrepressible human spirit.

We asked a hefty ticket price that night . . . and it took a lot of nerve, even on behalf of a lot of peace groups. Until it's remembered that in each and every month of a working life more is paid in tax to build a nuclear arsenal here in Britain. With the talent arrayed there were no carpers.

Here is much of that same talent in print, augmented by drawings from some of our best cartoonists who gave their work too. It's here to be enjoyed by a wider audience. These sketches can be played again – and they can stimulate new ones – in theatres, schools, village halls and the open air. The songs can be sung and heard again by other people. And the cartoons can festoon walls anywhere (Number Ten?), and speak to all kinds of ears.

'The Big One' was an affirmative show. This is an affirmative book, created by people who think that life is a great idea. We wanted our audience to feel that with us, to listen, to laugh and even to weep, then go away revitalised by the belief we share; that by the loudness of our voices, the force of our numbers, by the strength of our efforts in every field we can drive nuclear war back where it belongs – to the realm of the unthinkable, the realm of the impossible. So that by our will we can achieve peace, and a future, for ourselves, our children, our world.

We want that of our readers too . . .

Susannah York
Bill Bachle
1984

# British New World TV
ANTHONY MATHESON

Good evening. This is British New World Television, broadcasting from somewhere under England.

Well, it's just a week now since World War Three ended and British New World TV first went on the air. During that week, our viewing figures have shot up to an amazing 80% of the British population. Unfortunately the British population has gone down by 45%, so the increase doesn't show in the ratings. We're all jolly frustrated about that, I can tell you.

Now, before the news and weather, here is a repeat of the warning we broadcast earlier in the week.

In spite of the wonderful news that the War is over, do *not* go out on the streets to celebrate, as this could invalidate your life insurance policy; also, there *are* no streets. Remain in your inner shelter. We will let you know when it's safe to go out, should that situation ever arise.

That was a Government Health Warning.

Now, for those of you who *are* still with us, here is the weather forecast. London and the South-East will continue uninhabitable for the next seventy-five years or so. Temperatures, which have been rather high for the time of year, around 7,000 degrees Centigrade – that's 12,632 Fahrenheit – are now getting back to a more
seasonal level. In the rest of the country, some sunlight may be getting through but, if you do go outside, you'll still need to wrap up *very well indeed*.

That is the end of the weather forecast.

Here is the news.

The Prime Minister said today that the number of unemployed people in Britain has dropped rapidly in the last week and thousands more are dropping every day.

The United States President and the American survivors issued a statement today from their giant orbiting space station, saying they had been suffering from nausea. This was due to unevenness in the clockwise rotation of the station's artificial gravity system, and *not* to a guilt complex. Speaking from the Russian space station, the Russian Premier said that the American nausea was the inevitable result of their adherence to decadent, bourgeois, clockwise beliefs. He said that he was prepared to fight to defend the anti-clockwise ideas of the Russian station. The British Prime Minister said that if the British people had not been so unpatriotically lazy and selfish they could have built her a space station too.

Russia has announced that, during World War Three, a number of cruise missiles targeted on Moscow actually landed in a remote part of Siberia and failed to detonate. A team of scientists who examined one of the weapons discovered that it originated from the Greenham Common base and that the control circuits had been rendered inoperative by a pair of size nine knitting needles. The needles bore the name of Mrs Marie Lewis of Stourbridge in Worcestershire. The Russian Government said that Mrs Lewis had probably saved thousands of lives and expressed the personal gratitude of the Russian survivors; Sweden stated that she would be awarded the Nobel Peace Prize for an outstanding humanitarian act; the British Government announced that Mrs Lewis would be shot at half-past eight tomorrow morning. Mrs Lewis, in fact, died from the effects of fall-out two days ago.

That is the end of the news. Now here is a Motoring Flash.

We have just had a report that there is a motorist on the M5 Motorway near Bristol. The local RAC (the Radioactivity Control) are anxious to make contact with him before he makes contact with anybody else.

Ever since World War Three ended, survivor totals from all over the world have been fed into a computer here in London to discover who won. The final result is expected some time next Tuesday evening and we will be providing full coverage here on BNW TV. Robin Day will be analysing the results as they come in; Peter Snow will be standing by to record the megadeaths on the Swingometer, and Robert Kee will be asking Michael Heseltine if the nuclear deterrent can still be considered effective. That's next Tuesday here on BNW TV – the result of World War Three. Don't miss it.

Starting next Wednesday, a new phone-in series called 'Shut Up and Listen'. As the normal telephone system is no longer operating, a team of experts here in the studio will phone each other on our internal telephones and try to answer the questions you might be dying to ask – I do beg your pardon – the questions you might be eager to ask, if only you could contact the outside world. That's on Wednesday at 7.30 – 'Shut Up and Listen'.

Just starting now on Radio 4, 'The Archer'. And Phil is down to his last bottle of water. You're watching British New World Television . . .

Homines in aërem ejiciuntur, vel exuruntur.... *terribile est!*
*Men are blown up into the air, or are burnt.... it is terrible!*

# *Art Matters*

HOWARD BARKER

*A room in the National Gallery, with a table at which are seated three old men. They wear suits. Edging towards them holding either end of a framed masterpiece are two attendants. They wear overalls.*

**Bactus:** I am an extremely boring man. I have two children who care for me, but this could not have lasted. They would certainly have detected my boringness and had no more to do with me. I also have a wife who once loved me, but it was not a passion as I understand the word. It was affection; the coming together of frail temperaments in a rather hostile world. This also has deteriorated into something like routine, as it was bound to, given my capacity for boring people. I like a pint on Sunday mornings but, for obvious reasons, I drink alone – *(He trips.)* Sorry –

*They hold the canvas before the committee of old men.*

**Lesser:** I paint myself. I could have been a major artist – you may disagree with this – but my originality has been – shall we say – fucked by such close familiarity with all these geniuses. I think, if you know a genius, you ought to stay away from him – or her; you ought rather to seek isolation and, having found it, paint your arse off – as I would have done, had I been a free agent – painting away.
  I am particularly vulnerable to Titian – really, he completely – dare I say – fucks me – from the

perspective point of view. I cannot shake him off; his great monster of a brain – a sort of rape it is – of my integrity –

**1st Old Man:** Oh, ecstasy!

**2nd Old Man:** Hate it.

**1st Old Man:** Oh, ecstasy!

**3rd Old Man:** Haven't seen this for –

**2nd Old Man:** In store.

**3rd Old Man:** Years.

**2nd Old Man:** In store.

**1st Old Man:** Look at it and I go all – I go all –

**2nd Old Man:** Boys.

**1st Old Man:** No.

**2nd Old Man:** Boys.

**1st Old Man:** The thinness of the paint –

**2nd Old Man:** No. Boys.

**1st Old Man:** It is the transparent nature of the paint –

**3rd Old Man:** Sort of neo –

**2nd Old Man:** Neo-shit.

**3rd Old Man:** Not his best, there are six copies of this in –

**1st Old Man:** No, forgive me, not six copies –

**3rd Old Man:** Yes, six copies, Ralph –

**1st Old Man:** Not copies, versions –

**2nd Old Man:** Six whatevers of Boys Eating Grapes –

**3rd Old Man:** Red Star –

**1st Old Man:** Oh, not red, not red –

**2nd Old Man:** What's red?

**3rd Old Man:** Red is light protection against fall-out of under fifteen megatons. It is a shed in Wandsworth.

**1st Old Man:** Oh, not red! Silver!

**3rd Old Man:** Red. Next!

**Lesser:** Excuse me, may I come in here? I have spent six months standing under 'Boys with Grapes' and notwithstanding it is one of six versions, two of which are in the Metropolitan, one in the Hermitage, the others held privately in Surrey and Kuwait, I would seriously propose granting it a silver on the grounds that it –

**2nd Old Man:** Get it out.

**Lesser:** It –

**2nd Old Man:** No. Out, Frank.

**Lesser:** I HAVE STOOD UNDERNEATH THIS PICTURE FOR SIX MONTHS!

*Pause.*

**2nd Old Man:** Thank you for your unsolicited advice. We deem it unworthy of the Cotswold bunker –

**Lesser:** Oh, Del Sarto, look at that! The ankle, look, show me one quattrocento ankle painter that comes near that –

**1st Old Man:** Frank, it is the –

**Lesser:** Let it in the bunker, let it, guv!

*Pause.*

**3rd Old Man:** Frank, it is the decision of this committee that Del Sarto's 'Boys Eating Grapes' is not a priority worthy of preservation against direct hits of over fifteen megatons. It is not, in other words, Goya's 'Duke of Wellington'. I am sorry. This does not mean it will be destroyed. It may well be that artworks classified as red will escape all blast. I don't know. I am not prepared to speculate.

**Bactus:** Do you think of the day? I think of the day. I think how when we all are gone, and drifting in a thousand mile high column of microscopic dust, and there are no cities, and no buses, and no screaming kiddies in the playground, and no motorbikes in half-lit streets at night, I think of how the finest products of the European mind will be lying silent in the cavern known as Art One, airtight and dark, and when some vile mutant undoes the lock, milennia on milennia hence, it will point its snout at them and say, 'So this was them, the Europeans!' *(Pause.)* UGH!

**2nd Old Man:** Thank you, we are now six minutes behind. Remove it, please. We have five hundred pictures to judge between now and the Day called Blue, and Day called Blue being that on which forty pantechnicons will travel under escort to the bunker. Carry on. *(Bactus doesn't move.)* Carry on, I said.

*Pause.*

**3rd Old Man:** Michael, you have been here fifteen years, a very decent Grade Two Manual with prospects of a –

**Bactus:** I WANNA GO IN THE BUNKER.

*Pause.*

**3rd Old Man:** Come again –

**Bactus:** I WANNA GO IN THE BUNKER.

**2nd Old Man:** Don't be silly, the bunker is for –

**Bactus:** BEAUTY.

**2nd Old Man:** No, not –

**Bactus:** What, then?

**2nd Old Man:** You see, when we are dead – when you are dead – don't you think you will die happier in the knowledge that the civilisation of which you are a part –

**Bactus:** I WANNA GO IN THE BUNKER.

**3rd Old Man:** You aren't art!

**Bactus:** I AM ART.

*Pause.*

**1st Old Man:** He says he's art . . . .

**Bactus:** I am art. Look at my hand. Look at my fingers. Made by my mother, and improved by life. I'm art.

**1st Old Man:** There are something like eight hundred million white European male hands in this world. I do not think the market value – the cultural value – of your particular hand entitles it to a gold star guarantee of preservation, with all respect. If you were to get – and this is rather short notice, I appreciate – if you were to get, say, Francis Bacon to do a sketch of it, then I think I might say you could reasonably expect to see the sketch preserved, but the hand itself –

**Bactus:** Why do they draw things?

**3rd Old Man:** Who?

**Bactus:** Artists. Why?

**3rd Old Man:** Well, they do it because – *(Pause.)* I don't know why they do it – *(He looks at the others.)* Why do they?

**Lesser:** I have done a drawing. While you said all that. I have done a drawing called 'The Committee for the Preservation of European Culture reject the application from Manual Grade Two Bactus to be considered as a cultural artefact.' I would like to submit this drawing to be considered as a cultural artefact.

**2nd Old Man:** This is getting absurd –

**Lesser:** Please?

**Bactus:** I AM A BEAUTIFUL OBJECT! I AM A BEAUTIFUL OBJECT! I AM A BEAUTIFUL OBJECT!

# *Madman Theory of Deterrence*
DAVID HARE


*A man in his late forties comes on in a dark suit.*

Good evening. I am your new Minister of Defence. I will go batshit if anyone contradicts me. Don't contradict me.

Here tonight in a far-flung corner of the American Empire. . . .

I'm sorry, I will start again.

Voted in by an overwhelming majority of the people. . . .

Sorry.

Voted in by forty per cent of the seventy per cent of the people who bothered to vote, this government claims an overwhelming mandate. . . .

I will go batshit if anyone contradicts me.

The maintenance of freedom within a working democracy depends on the right to thorough and informed debate. Such free and unfettered debate must always take place in a big room just off Whitehall with a black front door guarded by white policemen. The public should remain behind crush barriers.

I have read some of the literature which opposes the government's firm commitment. . . .

Sorry.

I have read none of the literature which opposes the government's firm resolve to increase public expenditure by creating artificial jobs in the so-called boom sector of the economy, aptly called boom because. . . .

I will go batshit if anyone contradicts me.

Love, which was visited upon me, on a river-bank, by Henley, in the sun, with the sun beating down, in the late nineteen-forties, love which came to me with her in my arms, coming among the reeds and the riverbank, is the same love which informs the decisions of Her Majesty's Ministers.

Sorry.

Love, which has no place in affairs of state, belongs more properly to the reeds and riverbank, just outside Henley, where I fucked myself silly – I can show you the spot – in the late nineteen-forties.

Let me explain to you the madman theory of deterrence, invented by Richard Nixon fifteen years ago. The madman theory of deterrence rests on the idea that only a madman would use nuclear weapons, so in order to convince your enemy that you are contemplating their actual use, it is necessary to appear to be mad.

I am naked underneath this suit.

People often ask me, how does it feel to have the potential for blowing up the whole of Europe in your hands? Is it more interesting than your pre-vious work at the Ministry of the Environment? To this I reply, I do not have sole control. Nor indeed does my Prime Minister. She has dual control.

Let me explain to you the dual control madman theory of deterrence, invented by Margaret Thatcher last week. The dual control madman theory of deterrence rests upon the idea that some-where in the world there are two people mad enough to contemplate using nuclear weapons, and that these two people *admire* each other.

'How could a deterrent', says Margaret

Thatcher, '*be* a deterrent, unless one was willing to use it?'

She will go batshit if anyone contradicts her.

It is manly, yes, it is manly in the evenings to be seen about town with nuclear weapons. It is manly to go into restaurants and say, 'Serve me or I will destroy your restaurant with nuclear weapons.' It is mad and it is manly.

There is an enemy. Let us be in no doubt of this. There is an enemy out there which speaks with alien tongue and dresses in clothes which are ripped from the backs of sheep. They are longing to take over this country. They are longing to run British Rail and British Leyland. They want to sort out the problems of Northern Ireland. They are aching to get their hands on three million unemployed.

I am threatened with cuts. I am told that this country can no longer afford my programme of expenditure. But people cannot expect nuclear war on the cheap. They must be prepared to pay for it.

Her Majesty's Ministers have known love, grief, laughter, childbirth. The Prime Minister herself is a mother. . . .

Sorry.

The Prime Minister herself is a mother of two children, who have hearts, loins, and groins as we do, love as we do, breathe as I do, are totally insane as I am pretending to be. . . .

I will go batshit.

It is hard to earn a penny.

I have brown-nosed my way to this position and now I must sit round at Number Ten in the evenings and listen to the conversation of people who used to be socialists, now taking revenge on their youth by hanging their names round this government. I have to attend ceremonies at which dons of All Souls' and ex-editors of the *New Statesman* carve their initials on Polaris submarines. I have not to vomit.

I did not join the Tory Party for this. I joined to develop property and wear striped shirts, not to be lectured on morality by Intellectuals for Sale. Even I, the old slicker, I gag at this.

I am the saddest of all Her Majesty's Ministers but also the deepest. If I have to press the button, then it is true, yes, people will die, and in a way it will be a tragedy for them. But it is nothing as to my tragedy which is much greater, because I am a very interesting person.

I will give interviews on what it was like to be the person who did it. Everyone will be for me, or against me. Or dead.

I did not enter into politics to court cheap popularity.

I know that by letting everyone go on living I may garner a few cheap votes. We call that buying the electorate. It is against our deepest principles. On this, as on everything, we shall take the harder road, even if it means that we personally shall not be re-elected.

Thus it is today to be the Minister of Defence.

I will go batshit if anyone contradicts me.

## *Distance*

RIK MAYALL AND
ADE EDMONDSON
with additional material by
LISE MAYER

*Two men sit centre stage on deckchairs (facing audience)
as though gazing out to sea.*

**A:** Brian? . . . Brian? . . . sorry Trevor?

**B:** What?

**A:** Do you see that boat?

**B** *(opening eyes):* What – the green one or the blue one?

**A:** The turquoise one.

**B:** No . . . sorry, yes.

**A:** It's getting smaller.

**B:** That's because it's getting further away.

**A:** Exactly.

*Pause.*

**B:** How do you mean – 'Exactly'?

**A:** As the boat gets further and further away it gets
smaller and smaller . . . eventually it'll get so small
that it'll disappear.

**B:** What? You mean actually disappear?

**A:** Yes, actually.

**B:** But what about the people on the boat?

**A:** Well they'll disappear too.

**B:** But won't they notice that it's getting smaller and jump off while the going's good?

**A:** No. Because as the boat gets smaller and smaller they get just as small – in proportion. They won't notice they're getting any smaller . . . and eventually they won't be able to notice anything at all because . . . they won't be there.

*Pause.*

**B:** Bollocks.

**A:** Where?

**B:** You're talking bollocks.

**A:** I haven't got any talking bollocks.

**B:** Listen: my Auntie Reenie went to Majorca for her holidays last year, and when she came back she was exactly the same size – *(makes a gesture implying that she is about two feet tall.)*

**A:** All right, all right – if you don't believe me, go over there and try it for yourself. *(Gestures towards audience.)*

**B:** All right then, I will.

*He gets up and walks towards audience. He falls into orchestra pit (or goes downstairs to audience).*

**A:** See what I mean?

**B:** God, you're right, you're only this big *(he holds his thumb and forefinger up to show size).*

***A** also holds fingers up,. but wider apart. They compare sizes.*

**B:** How does it work then?

**A** *(pleased to be asked)*: Well it's very simple Beverly . . . sorry, Trevor. It's very simple indeed.

**B:** Oh, good.

**A:** Now – have you ever thought about Italian people?

**B:** No.

**A:** Oh, all right then – well, what do you notice about Italian people that's different to us English people?

**B:** They speak Italian.

**A:** No.

**B:** Yes they do.

**A:** Yes but no – what else do you notice about them?

**B:** They eat spaghetti.

**A:** No.

**B** *(angry)*: They do!

**A** *(shouts)*: All right, I'll tell you – look: they're *smaller* than us.

**B:** Oh I *see* – so what you're saying is – correct me if I'm wrong – as you go further round the universe, towards Italy, things get smaller.

**A:** That's right. And not only as far as Italy – you go to Pakistan and they're even smaller.

**B:** You go to Japan, they're bloody tiny!

**A:** That's right – you go all the way to New Guinea and what do you get? Pygmies! That's why if you go all the way round the world, and a bit out – to the moon – the people are so tiny you can't see them at all.

**B:** No – I've seen the Americans on the moon – I've seen it on the telly.

**A:** Ah well, yes, you see, that's because as you go the other way round the world from England things get bigger. I mean, who's the biggest people in the world?

**B:** The Texans.

**A:** Texans, absolutely, John Wayne, Ronald Reagan. . . .

**B:** Nancy Reagan.

**A:** That's why the Americans can send a Texan to the moon and he'll get smaller all right on the way but not so small that he'll disappear.

**B:** Small enough to fit on the telly!

**A:** Absolutely.

**B:** That's probably why there are so many American programmes on the telly.

**A:** That's right – they travel well. I mean, that's why the Russians have never landed anyone on the moon. They send loads of them up there but they all disappear half way. Space is full of microscopic invisible Russians.

**B:** Which is why the Russians make such good spies.

**A:** Yes, and why the Americans can never prove that they're there. It's a very dangerous situation.

**B:** I don't think that a microscopic invisible Russian four million light years away is much of a danger.

**A:** That's because you're stupid.

**B:** How does all this work then?

**A:** Air pressure.

**B:** Hair pressure?

**A:** No – *air* pressure.

**B:** How do you mean?

**A:** Well, you see the universe is very, very big and the universe is full of planets. . . . Big ones . . . little ones. . . .

**B:** In-betweeny-ones.

**A:** And all those planets –

**B:** Green ones. . . .

**A:** Yes, and all those planets –

**B:** Yellow ones.

**A:** Yes, yes and all those planets –

**B:** Green and yellow ones. . . .

**A:** All kinds of fucking planets all right? And all those planets must be held up there by something – otherwise the Earth would be flattened in a rain of planets. And what do you think is holding all those planets up?

**B:** I don't know.

**A:** Ah, but I do.

**B:** Well what did you ask me for?

**A:** That's not important. . . . What do you think is holding all the planets up?

**B:** I DON'T KNOW!

**A:** AIR! All those planets are held up there by columns of air *(gestures)* – rather like a golf tee.

**B:** Well, how does that make people get smaller the further you get away?

**A:** This is where it gets interesting.

**B:** Oh, good.

**A** *(standing up – he is getting carried away)*: You see, over America there's only a tiny planet – I don't know which one it is . . . Mercury, I think . . . or Pluto.

**B:** Goofy.

**A:** That's him. Goofy is hovering over America, and he's only a small planet as we know, so the pressure of air in the column of air that's holding him up is only small. It's very light, you see, so there's not much pressure on the Americans' heads and they can grow up very tall *(demonstrates)*. Whereas over Japan there's a massive great planet, the size of Uranus, and all that's weighing down the air very heavily on the Japanese's heads. *(Demonstrates a Japanese person being squashed down.)* That's why they're all very small.

**B:** I've just realised, right, why the Japanese economy is booming. Well, they only have to make things very, very small: like cars, I mean – they're titchy-dinky cars. And what does a dinky car cost?

**A** *(instantly)*: Sixty-eight pence.

**B:** About that – yes. And then they export the dinky cars over to this country and they get big enough for us to get into and we pay thousands for them!

**A:** Bastards! And the Americans have got huge great cars – Cadillacs, Fords – you look at a Ford when it gets to this country and it's nothing – an Escort or something.

**B:** Hey, Brian?

**A:** What?

**B:** You know that boat?

**A:** Well?

**B:** It has disappeared.

# On the Beach at Cambridge

ADRIAN MITCHELL

I am Assistant to the Regional Commissioner
At Block E, Brooklands Avenue;
Communications Centre for Region 4,
Which used to be East Anglia.

I published several poems as a young man
But later found I could not meet my own high
   standards
So tore up all my poems and stopped writing.
(I stopped painting at eight and singing at five).
I was seconded to Block E
From the Ministry for the Environment.

Since there are no established poets available
I have come out here in my MPC,
(Maximum Protective Clothing),
To dictate some sort of poem or word-picture
Into a miniature cassette recorder.

When I first stepped out of Block E on to this
   beach
I could not record any words at all.
So I chewed two of the orange-flavoured pills
They give us for morale, switched on my Sony
And recorded this:

I am standing on the beach at Cambridge.
I can see a group in their MPC
Pushing Hoover-like and Ewbank-like machines
Through masses of black ashes.

The taller men are soldiers or police,
The others, scientific supervisors.
This group moves slowly across what seems
Like an endless car park with no cars at all.

I think that, in one moment,
All the books in Cambridge
Leapt off their shelves,
Spread their wings
And became white flames
And then black ash.
And I am standing on the beach at Cambridge.

You're a poet, said the Regional Commissioner,
Go out and describe that lot.

The University Library – a little hill of brick-dust.
King's College Chapel – a dune of stone-dust.
The sea is coming closer and closer.

The clouds are edged with green.
They are sagging low under some terrible weight.
They move more rapidly than usual.

Some younger women with important jobs
Were admitted to Block E
But my wife was a teacher in her forties.
We talked it over
When the nature of the crisis became apparent.
We agreed someone had to carry on.
That day I kissed her goodbye as I did every day
At the door of our house in Chesterton Road.
I kissed my son and my daughter goodbye.
I drove to Block E beside Hobson's Brook.
I felt like a piece of paper
Being torn in half.

And I am standing on the beach at Cambridge.
Some of the men in their MPC
Are sitting on the ground in the black ashes.
One is holding his head in both his hands.

I was forty-two three weeks ago.
My children painted me
Bright-coloured cards with poems for my
   birthday.
I stuck them with Blue-tack on the kitchen door.
I can remember the colours.

But in one moment all the children in Cambridge
Spread their wings
And became white flames
And then black ash.

And the children of America, I suppose.
And the children of Russia, I suppose.

And I am standing on the beach at Cambridge
And I am watching the broad black ocean tide
Bearing on its shoulders a burden of black ashes.

And I am listening to the last words of the sea
As it beats its head against the dying land.

ANGER                                    YOUENS

War

Youens

# *Precisely*
HAROLD PINTER

*Two men at a table with drinks. Silence.*

**Stephen:** I mean, we've said it time and time again, haven't we?

**Roger:** Of course we have.

**Stephen:** Time and time again. Twenty million. That's what we've said. Time and time again. It's a figure supported by facts. We've done our homework. Twenty million is a fact. When these people say thirty I'll tell you exactly what they're doing – they're distorting the facts.

**Roger:** Scandalous.

**Stephen:** Quite. I mean, how the hell do they *know*?

**Roger:** Quite.

**Stephen:** We've done the *thinking*.

**Roger:** Quite.

**Stephen:** That's what we're paid for.

**Roger:** Paid a bloody lot too.

**Stephen:** Exactly. Good money for good brains.

*They drink.*

**Stephen:** Thirty million! I mean. . .!

**Roger:** Exactly.

**Stephen:** I'll tell you, neither I nor those above me are going to put up with it much longer. These people, Roger, these people are actively and wilfully deceiving the public. Do you take my point?

**Roger:** I'd put the bastards up against a wall and shoot them.

**Stephen:** As a matter of fact, I've got a committee being set up to discuss that very thing.

**Roger:** Really? Well done.

> *They drink.*

**Roger:** Actually . . . I've heard that they're talking about forty million.

**Stephen:** What!

**Roger:** And one or two of them . . . have taken it even further.

**Stephen:** What do you mean?

**Roger:** Oh . . . you know . . . fifty . . . sixty . . . seventy. . . .

**Stephen:** But that's almost the whole population!

**Roger:** I know.

**Stephen:** Well, I'm buggered.

**Roger:** It's a bit of a bloody cheek, isn't it, Stephen?

**Stephen:** It's more than a bloody cheek, Roger.

**Roger:** Indeed.

> *Pause.*

**Stephen:** You know what I'm going to recommend we do with these people?

**Roger:** What?

**Stephen:** I'm going to recommend that they be hung, drawn and quartered. I want to see the colour of their entrails.

**Roger:** Same colour as the Red Flag, old boy.

**Stephen:** Quite.

*They drink.*

**Stephen:** You see, what makes this whole business doubly disgusting is that the citizens of this country are behind us. They're ready to go with us on the twenty million basis. They're perfectly happy! And what are they faced with from these bastards? A deliberate attempt to subvert and undermine their security. And their faith.

*Roger drinks and then looks at Stephen.*

**Roger:** Give me another two, Stephen.

*Stephen stares at him.*

**Stephen:** Another two?

**Roger:** Another two million. And I'll buy you another drink. Another two for another drink.

**Stephen** *(slowly)*: No, no, Roger. It's twenty million. Dead.

**Roger:** You mean precisely?

**Stephen:** I mean dead. Precisely. *(Pause.)* I want you to accept that figure. *(Pause.)* Accept the figure.

*They stare at each other.*

**Roger:** Twenty million, dead, precisely?
**Stephen:** Precisely.

Elvis Costello
Peacemongering at the
Victoria Apollo  11:30 am
rehearsal
18·12·83

John Jensen.

# *Peace in our Time*★

ELVIS COSTELLO

Out of the aeroplane stepped Chamberlain,
With a condemned man's stare
But we all cheered wildly, a photograph was
    taken,
As he waved a piece of paper in the air.

Now the disco machine lives in Munich
And we are all friends and I slip on my Italian
    dancing shoes
As the evening descends.

And the bells take their toll,
Once again, in a victory chime.
And we can thank God that we've finally got
Peace in our time.

There's a man goin' round taking names,
No matter who you claim to be.
As innocent as babies,
A mad dog with rabies, you're still a part of
    some conspiracy.

Meanwhile there's a light over the ocean,
Burning brighter than the sun.
And a man sits alone in a bar
And says, 'Oh God what have we done?'

And the bells, take their toll,
Once again, in victory chime.
And we can thank God that we've finally got
Peace in our time.

★ *The music for this song is at the back of the book.*

They're lighting a bonfire, upon every hilltop in
    the land.
Just another tiny island invaded,
When he's got the whole world in his hands.
And the heavy-weight champion fights
In the international propaganda star wars.

There's already one spaceman in the White House,
What d'you want another one for?

And the bells take their toll,
Once again, in a victory chime.
And we can thank God that we've finally got
Peace in our time.

# I Know the Feeling

EMMA THOMPSON

Hello.

This is lovely, isn't it? It's warm for once! Don't often get balmy nights in England. Very unusual! Lovely. I like that one over there . . . in the silver frame. Nice sort of blue effect don't you think?

I'm terribly sorry, I don't know your name. . . .

Ho Piet Minh??

Oh, it's Vietnamese, I see. I'm Margery. . . . That's nice, isn't it? Are you a boat person?

Oh, how exciting – I've never met – um. . . . How was the journey?

Yes, I can imagine. It's such a terribly long way, isn't it? I crewed once on a yacht and got terribly sea-sick. It was awful. I wanted to die. Did you see that documentary the other day? About Vietnam?

Oh. No, nor did I. But I hear it was awfully good. You know, very accurate.

Belinda? Belinda!! You simply must meet um . . . Ho . . . oh, sorry – Minh. He's from Vietnam. We were just talking about that awfully good documentary they had. . . . Hasn't he got a lovely smile?!

Yes, I'd love another, thank you.

How do you find it here? London's awfully expensive, isn't it? Do you like the food? What do you eat?

Gosh . . . I haven't had baked beans for ages, but they're really very good, aren't they? Is it very different food-wise where you are, or were, rather?

Yes . . . yes . . . yes. It's awful going hungry, isn't it? I remember from when I had glandular fever. Awful.

Your English is awfully good, you know. I'm afraid I don't speak a word of Vietnamese . . . dreadful, I know, but they don't teach it at school. Isn't that embarrassing? Well, I suppose there aren't that many people who speak Vietnamese. . . . What's it like? Vietnamese. Say something.

Oh, no. Go on, say something.

Oh, I don't know. What a nice evening or something.

Oh, it's lovely! Sounds just like Chinese.

No, I don't speak Chinese either, I'm afraid, just 'O'-Level French. Comment ça va? and that sort of thing.

Do you have any children?

Eight!

Gosh, that is a handful. . . . Are they all here?

Oh, no! You didn't have to leave them behind? How awful! It's dreadful when you have to go away without them, isn't it? I remember when Nigel and I went to Florence, we had to leave ours with a tame aunt and it was heart-breaking going out of that door and seeing their little faces at the window. They were *convinced* we were never going to come back . . . sweet. Who's looking after yours?

Gosh . . . yes. I had a friend who put her child into care and it was very painful for her, but they were very well looked after and it turned out for the best in the end.

She's in advertising now. What do you do? Do you have a job?

What, these?

AND MAN DISCOVERED FIRE

THE BUTTON
DANGER
DO NOT PRESS

You mean you painted them?

Oh. Gosh. How embarrassing. You must forgive me. I simply hadn't thought of you as a. . . .

# Count-down
JOHN BENCH

*Suburban bedroom – in other words one bed and one
wardrobe. A woman **Kate** – a little housewife – and her
lover **Tom** are on the bed necking. The radio is on
playing classical music. The music stops but they take no
notice of the following announcement.*

**Radio:** We interrupt this programme of chamber music
to bring the news that talks to avoid the ultimate
nuclear confrontation have broken down and that
nuclear missiles have been launched. The four-
minute count-down has just begun. Here are the
details. The violin was played by Vladimir. . . .

*They switch the radio off.*

**Tom:** Who cares?

**Kate:** Oh, Tom, I think this is the way I'd like to go.

**Tom:** Kate, are you sure that Jim is still at the office?

*There is a bang at the door.*

**Jim** *(off)*: Hell, what's this door doing locked?
*(Knocking.)* Kate, are you in there?

**Kate** *(sotto)*: My husband. Quick – in the cupboard.
*(She shouts:)* We're not decent – I mean, I'm not
decent.

*She hustles **Tom** into the cupboard. **Tom** protesting,
pointing at his watch and the radio.*

**Jim** *(off)*: The four-minute warning's gone.

> **Kate** lets him in. **Jim** *rushes in stripping off and leads her to the bed.*

**Jim:** All ready I see – good thinking old girl.

**Kate:** Oh, no, Jim – not now, it seems wrong in the middle of the afternoon.

**Jim:** Look the world's going to end in about three and a half minutes and I want to go out in an orgasmic ecstasy and be gone before the remorse sets in. Come on, we can cut down the foreplay if you like and we might just have time for the cigarette.

**Kate:** Oh, Jim, I thought you'd given up smoking.

**Jim:** All right. I've been sneaking a few. It hardly matters now. What's the matter with you?

**Kate:** I see. Well, that is very honest of you. I think this is a good time for honesty. A time to be completely open with each other.

**Jim:** Yes, yes.

**Kate:** A time to share our secrets.

**Jim:** Of course, of course, now come on.

**Kate:** To spend our last few moments with the person one loves.

**Jim:** Of course, of course, that's why I'm here.

**Kate:** A time for total openness between us.

**Jim:** For heaven's sake.

**Kate:** Good.

*She goes to the cupboard, opens it and lets* **Tom** *out.*

**Kate:** Jim, I would like you to meet Tom.

**Tom:** How do you do?

> **Jim** *looks in amazement at* **Tom** *and also at his watch. The sketch gathers speed from here on to its frenetic finish.*

**Kate:** Now, I know this will come as a shock to you, Jim, but I want you to know I've been making enquiries into a quickie divorce.

> **Jim** *is looking at his watch.*

**Jim:** How quick do you want it, for heaven's sake?

**Kate:** Our relationship hasn't been everything it should have been so I turned to someone who doesn't think of me as just a body but appreciates my taste in bedroom wallpaper.

**Jim:** Oh, this is terrific, this is. I've got three minutes to live and I break my neck to get here to be with my wife – if I'd known, I would have stayed at the office with Miss Leverage in the Duplicating Room.

**Kate:** Now this is no time for spiteful retribution, it's a moment for calm. Who is Miss Leverage?

**Jim:** Oh, yes, two can play at this game. As it happens I have never made so much as a move to suggest that. . . .

> *They hear a female voice.*

**Sally** *(off)*: Mr Davies, Mrs Davies.

>**Sally** *bursts in.*

**Kate:** Who is this?

**Jim:** Miss Leverage, what are you doing out of duplicating? This isn't lunch hour.

**Sally:** Oh, call me Sally. Life is too short for last names. I had to come. I followed you home. I wanted to spend my last moments with you. It was one and a half minutes to my boyfriend's, two to you – so I thought long term.

**Jim:** Miss Leverage. Sally. I had no idea . . . but. . . . This isn't right.

**Sally:** It is too late for right and wrong. I knew you would run home to be with your wife and I wanted to save you from a terrible cliché.

**Jim:** My word you're right. Of course, it's a cliché. I shouldn't have come here, I should have stayed with you in duplicating and forced myself upon you on top of the Mitre 1500 in lunch hour and together we would have been devoured by the shredder, but I thought that was just a fantasy.

**Sally:** But, Mr Davies. Jim. We only have two and a half minutes to live – we can have our fantasies.

**Tom:** Oh, it's all coming out tonight, isn't it?

**Kate:** We'll talk about this later.

**Jim:** There is no later.

**Kate:** Come on, Tom, let's start again.

**Tom:** No, Sally's right, Jim's right. It's just a terrible cliché that I should want to spend my last few minutes in the arms of the other woman. It's so corny. It's just not what I thought I'd do if I knew I didn't have long to live.

**Kate:** Well, it's too late to start writing *War and Peace*.

**Tom:** I'd rather. . . .

**Kate:** Let's hear it.

**Tom:** I'd like to die scoring a winning goal for Liverpool in a Cup Final. Having just knocked out Sylvester Stallone and beaten the world record for the mile and then had a shower with Bo Derek in a wet suit.

**Sally:** And me.

**Tom:** What, you too?

**Sally:** No, I too have a fantasy. Water ski-ing naked, like Botticelli's Venus, on a scallop drawn by four dolphins to glide out on to a blue horizon and be swallowed by the sun, to the sounds of . . . oh, heaven.

**Jim:** To the sounds of what?

**Sally:** Barry Manilow singing 'If I should love again'. There, I've said it. *(She breaks down.)* How can you ever speak to me again? *(All supportive.)* There, there.

**Jim:** Miss Leverage, I wonder if I could fondle your shoes?

**Kate:** Yes, yes. You're all right. I too have a secret longing. I want to be dominated by a Prussian Hussar, like the one who strays into your garden after a Badedas bubble bath. I imagine I keep him

locked up in a cupboard somewhere so that I can
get him out from time to time and dust his medals
down, polish his creaking leather work while he
beats me with the *Good Food Guide.*

**Jim:** I like it. I like it.

**Tom:** . . . a Dry Cane in one hand and Brooke Shields
in the other holding a pumpkin.

**Sally:** Oh, I feel wonderful now that my secret is out.
Now that you all know. You are all my friends, I
love you all.

**Tom:** Me too. I am purged of all guilt.

**Jim:** And me. I feel so relieved.

**Kate:** Suddenly, yes, I love you all too, just as much as
my Prussian Hussar.

**Jim:** We must do this again.

*They all embrace and break down.*

**Jim:** Thirty seconds to go. Shouldn't we be singing
'Auld Lang Syne' or something?

*They take hands for 'Auld Lang Syne'.*

**Kate:** Yes. There should be Big Ben or something on
the radio.

*She turns it on.*

**Radio:** . . . and that is the end of the close of play
scores, which brings us up to the news. Owing to
an eleventh hour breakthrough in the negotiations
between the superpowers, all enemy missiles

aimed at European capitals have been recalled. The end of the world will not take place.

*They turn the radio off. There is silence. The four break the 'Auld Lang Syne' links and there is a moment's silence in which they resume their previous positions and start spitting accusations at each other.*

Rat!
Pervert!
Two-timer!
Bitch!
Jezebel!
Home breaker!
Marriage wrecker!
Barry Manilow, indeed!
A pumpkin!
Shoes, is it?

*During the fracas the door of the cupboard opens and a gleaming Prussian Hussar★ in full ceremonial dress and carrying the* Good Food Guide *sneaks out behind them and skulks from the room hoping not to be seen.*

*Blackout.*

★ *We had Elvis Costello. Pick your own Aunt Sally! Eds.*
  *(Sorry, Elvis!)*

# Glowboy

STEPHEN LOWE

He would have been lit anyway.
The full moon and the hard-packed snow

he was followed by a wake
of browning slush.

we watched him, through ice on window
we were tired
tending the fading fire
measuring stores against each present flame.

my wife opened the door, and beckoned him
    enter.
I'm sure I would have done so just a moment later.
he turned his face towards her
the flames around him flickered
his glow reflected in his own futile
pool of water.

He entered.
we sat him by the fire as one does with guests
and were silent
as one is with guests in these parts

he was a child
my son I called him though I never spoke it.
'Help me,' he said
he wished it in the name of hospitality

The heat he gave us was warm and soothing
diamonds on the windows
transformed to dew
moistening the room
breathing became easy
I drank in mouthfuls
as with harvest beer
the fire died in envy

'Help me.'
'How can we help?' I said.
'I am burning.'

There were no burns upon him.
Better than to freeze to death.
'Count your blessings,' I said.
We have learnt to accept so much.
What else can you teach a child?
'You would have frozen out there
without this miracle.'

'Help me,' he said. 'I am burning.'
I shook my head. Children see only the present
    pain
never the wider shape of suffering and sacrifice
My wife
touched my lips as I began to speak
her fingers burnt with what I always imagined
passion would be
I almost forgot the child
in the sudden urge to embrace
without the struggle to preserve the coverings.
(Love in this climate is always the choice
of which part to leave freezing –
the glow never quite makes the whole anatomy –
or if it ever did, I forget.

in winter summer is only a wild yearning
for the clearly impossible)

she guided my face to watch him
a tear in his eye moving slowly down
never made his cheek
before bubbling away.

He was burning. I knew it.
I could not deny it, having
seen it with my own eyes,
felt it with my body.
'How can this be?' I said.

'Help me.'

My wife was weeping,
warm for the first time and
weeping
her tears moving freely
within the laws
of gravity

'GOD', she cried.
her eyes touching his flames –
I understood her.
How can you thank Him
and curse Him at the same time?
It must be a failure
in our understanding.

'Help me.'

'Do you want the fire put out?'

My wife never spoke
sometimes she is most unhelpful

she moves towards him
her skin red and bloated
she could not reach him.

We had only ice to offer
and that he turned to air
for the fire to feed on

'Have you visited others?' I said
'Someone must know the answer.
There's a wise man over the hill.'

'That was the way he came,'
my wife reminded me.
What else can I say?

Silence.

He rose and left us
this child who should have run in all directions
walked doggedly away
like an extinguished man

My wife stood in the doorway
I watched him through the diamonds as they
    reformed
until there were hundred
glowboys
on the far horizon.

'Close the door.'

We sat, but it was difficult to gain the energy
to rekindle.
My wife wept.
Her tears turned to ice and cut her cheeks.

I understood
We had truly wished to help the boy.
What can anybody do?

I missed the warmth.

# The Russian Premier

ANDREW MARSHALL
& DAVID RENWICK

*We start with a voice over announcement. During its duration a platform is wheeled onto the stage. It contains a small lectern draped with a red flag, and the hammer and sickle. Behind is standing the Russian Premier, rigidly, as if he is attached to a pole set in the platform. The men in white coats tend him, one wheeling the platform centre stage and lifting the stiff inert figure off, the other playing out a length of electric flex which disappears into his charge's heavy greatcoat. They leave.*

**Voice over announcement:** Ladies and gentlemen. Konstantin Chernenko, President and Premier of the USSR, General Secretary of the Communist Party, holder of the Stalin Peace Prize (runner up), the Rasputin Cross (first class), the Karl Marx Shield for the Most Promising Newcomer to the Kremlin 1983, the Trotsky all-comers Ice Pick Trophy and a Crackerjack Pencil.

*A whine and flash of electric arc from the wings as he jerks into life abruptly.*

*He blinks at his papers and begins:*

**Chernenko:** Good evening. I am very pleased to be invited here tonight on this occasion. To see so many people gathered without recourse to gunpoint makes me glad to be alive.

Indeed, it makes me surprised to be alive. But

this is no time for philosophy; I am here to talk about Russia. Russia is a great country, and a happy country.

Food riots – what are they? Meat shortages – never heard of them. See this? *(He gets out a packet of crisps.)* A packet of crisps.

And that's not the only one we've got, believe me. Also, we have Pork Scratchings – dozens of them! In fact, most meals in Russia are unusually lavish. I, myself, am so immune to the pangs of hunger I often find I really have to force something down. As anyone who has ever flown in our airspace will have noticed.

The Warsaw Pact is a most happy organisation. All right, so we have to exercise a little . . . discipline from time to time, but that is harmless. Let me give you an example: you know how when a little schoolboy has been naughty in class you have to admonish him with an injection of sodium pentathol? Well, it is just the same with our member countries when they commit an unfortunate error and have to be corrected. Stories of Soviet aggression are laughable.

Ha, ha, ha.

You know, I find it quite inexplicable that, whenever I send a few of our tank divisions to pick flowers on the Polish border, you make a big issue of it and say we are flexing our muscles. Of course we are not. Although we could, if we wished, because it is a well-known fact that Russia's athletes are the best in the world. And that is true if they are male or female. Which, of course, most of them are. All right, so our Women's Shot Putt champion shaves twice a day. So what? Unsightly hair on the knuckles can detract from a woman's femininity. Anyway, I am drifting from the point.

I want to assure you personally today that none of those in Russia who regard our Nuclear Arms Strategy as provocative are mistreated. I myself visited the new National Institute of Psychology in Omsk only the other year and it is a happy place. Many of the inmates spend large portions of the day just laughing. And I can tell you I was pleased to visit many distinguished members of the peace movement and shake them warmly by the foot.

It is true, however, that, with no encouragement from me, our talented scientists continue to develop many horrifying devices in the name of progress. This they do willingly, for the love of their intellect, for the love of their homeland and for the love of their testicles. And I can tell you that we are not falling behind with technology either. The Soviet Union has long since mastered the microchip and is building bigger ones every year. Also, in Russia we have managed to eliminate the single biggest cause of death. Old age.

Yes, Russia is a great country. And I say that with no personal motives whatsoever, so there is no question of bias.

Above all, Russia is a jolly country. A country completely without fear. A country where a man can live his whole life with no worry whatsoever that his upper molars may someday be wired to an electric sanding drill. If you don't believe me – why don't you come and visit us? Better still, we'll come and visit you.

Goodnight.

**Ronald Reagan**
Born Grantham, Illinois
1826

Renowned as the youthful
star of such epics as
'Bathtime for Bumbo' and
'Paint Your Hair On!',
Ronald Reagan subsequently
became front man for a
group of Californian
businessmen with political
ambitions, calling
themselves 'The Winged
Psychos of Destiny to Stomp
Out Godless Pink Subversion
Today League', now known
more succinctly as the
'Kitchen Cabinet'.

Reagan's administration
has been most notable for
the calibre of his advisers,
the foremost among these
being William P. Clark and
Francis the Talking Mule.
His interests include getting
good shut-eye and eating
regular.

# Ban the Bomb ★

IAN DURY

Wrap yourself in silver paper
Put a sandbag on your head
Crawl inside your fall–out shelter
Underneath your garden shed.

Boil an egg
Or have a cuddle
Cut your toenails
Make the bed,
By the time
This record's finished
Everybody will be dead.

*Chorus*
Ban the bomb
Ban the bomb
Ban the bomb
Ban the bomb

For those who do not wish to die
Raise up your voices to the sky
And sing away the missiles

Wash your smalls
Feed the cactus
Telephone your Uncle Fred
By the time
This record's finished
Everybody will be dead.

★ *The music for this song is at the back of the book.*

# *Elevenses*

JOHNNY SPEIGHT

*Two working-class ladies drift in with mops and buckets and roll-your-own fags from stage left and mopping and stopping and puffing make their way across the stage to exit stage right.*

**Min:** . . . No . . . what my Bert says is, it's no good the Government sitting up there in that bloody Houses of Parliament, going on about who they like and who they don't like. . . . They sit up there and start bloody wars they can't afford . . . and then they come on the earhole to us and expect us to pay for 'em. I mean, look at that old fool, Chamberlain, with that last bloody war we had . . . the one we had with Hitler. . . . Peace in our time, he says, and hardly a month later he's back on the wireless. . . . No undertaking having been given His Majesty's Government has no alternative but to declare war on Germany. . . . Didn't give a thought to the cost of it, did he? Oh, no. My Bert says didn't enter his head to go into a few figures . . . get an estimate. . . . Oh, no. . . .

**Vi:** My Wally's always going into figures.

**Min:** Yes, I know.

**Vi:** They shouldn't start wars if they can't afford 'em. . . .

**Min:** 'Course they shouldn't. They should be made to do what the rest of us have to do when we want something we can't afford . . . save up for it. . . .

**Vi:** Or do what the Jews do – have a six-day war.

**Min:** Be a lot cheaper. . . .

**Vi:** Well, I mean, you wouldn't have to go out and buy so many missiles and bombs for a six-day war, would you?

**Min:** For six days you could hire 'em. . . .

**Vi:** . . . and send back what you didn't need. . . .

**Min:** Sale or return. What I'd like to know . . . what's wrong with the old bomb we had? The one we dropped on the Japs? That was a good bomb, wasn't it? Eh? There was nothing wrong with that bomb was there? That made a big enough bang, didn't it?

**Vi:** It was good enough for the Japs. . . .

**Min:** Good enough for anyone, I should think. . . .

**Vi:** If it was good enough for the Japs it's good enough for the Russians, I say. . . .

**Min:** Any old bomb's good enough for them, I should think. And they're talking about making a clean bomb for 'em now. . . .

**Vi:** I bet they wouldn't do that for us. . . .

**Min:** And we shouldn't do it for them either . . . drop a dirty bomb on 'em, a dirty bomb's good enough for the Russians. . . . Dirty swines. . . .

**Vi:** What I say is what's wrong with all them germs we had we was gonna drop on the Russians?

**Min:** There you are. . . . Money wasted, wasn't it? All that money we spent on germ warfare, and what's happened to it? Wasted. Never used.

**Vi:** And yer poison gas.

**Min:** And yer mustard gas. . . . What's wrong with using that on yer Russians?

**Vi:** Nothing that I can see. . . .

**Min:** I can't see why we didn't drop one of them old atom bombs on the Russians the same time we dropped it on the Japs, it'd been a lot cheaper to have done it then.

**Vi:** We couldn't then, could we?

**Min:** Why not? You have to fly past Russia to get to Japan.

**Vi:** But the Russians was our friends then, wasn't they?

**Min:** They was only our friends while we was fighting the Japs and the Germans, they've never been our real friends, they was only wartime friends, that's all they was. No . . . we should've dropped that bomb on 'em then and been done with it. . . .

YOUENS.

- SKYRAPERS -

# *Optimistic Poem*
TERRY JOHNSON

Being hit by the bomb
Remember this
Being hit by the bomb
Is nothing more and nothing less
Than being hit by a bloody big bus

Except that it happens to you
And someone else
And everyone else too.

So remember this
We could all be knocked down by a bomb
   tomorrow.
Remember that
Because that's the positive side to the bomb.


Here's a game you can play at home
It's called 'Go Bang in the Head'
It works like this:

Whatever you're doing during the course of an
   ordinary day
If you happen to notice your heart's not full of joy
Let the bomb go bang in your head.

Let the bomb go bang in your head
To remind you what making love is

Let the bomb go bang in your head
Next time wood seems ordinary

Let the bomb go bang in your head
Next time red looks simple
Next time you forget that water's wet.

Let the bomb go bang in your head
Next time you eat an egg while talking on the
telephone.

Let the bomb go bang in your head
Like a clout from the stick of a wise old master

Let the bomb go bang in your head
Next time you watch 'Brideshead Revisited'

Let the bomb go bang in your head
Next time you see your mother or your father
And can't think of a single thing to say

Let the bomb go bang in your head
Next time your lover betrays you with a man
called Ian

Let the bomb go bang in your head
Next time you decide to get up in an hour or so

Let the bomb go bang in your head
Next time you decide you won't because you can't
afford it

Let the bomb go bang in your head
Next time you feel like being alive a bit for a few
seconds

And keep going bang in your head
Until you're alive a lot forever


And remember
There *is* a positive side to the bomb.

This side of it.

THATCHER'S MONUMENT.

# *Nuclear Fall-out*★

ALAN BENCE

*Three pig-tailed schoolgirls sitting under heavily sand-bagged kitchen table.*

If the Russians send over a missile
Which explodes you can still stay alive,
If you read all the Government pamphlets
You will learn to protect and survive.
It's such fun knowing someone's really thinking,
Yes, it's fun how somebody really cares,
And it's fun knowing it will never happen,
'Cos no-one would really dare.
We just love nuclear fission
And our great politicians –
We just love having nuclear fall-out.

So we read all the books and the papers –
Well you know just in case don't know why,
It's a bloody good job that we did though,
'Cos next day there's a bomb in the sky.
It's such fun though we're threatened with
    extinction,
It's such fun knowing we will be all right,
And it's fun knowing tho' we are protected,
It still gave us such a fright.
We just love all this waiting,
While our fate they're debating –
We just love having nuclear fall-out.

So we brought loads of food and some water
And we sandbagged the walls like they said,

★ The music for this song is at the back of the book.

Then we sat 'neath the stairs like they told us –
They were right we're OK we're not dead,
'Cos it's fun sitting in here all together,
Yes it's fun knowing we will all get through,
And it's fun that the gen'rals have assured us
Everything they say is true.
We just love jolly notions
Of some nuclear explosions –
We just love having nuclear fall-out.

So we were, just us three in this shelter,
We were having a wonderful day;
I was sick, so was I, I was burning
But we thought what the hell anyway.
'Cos it's fun having radiation sickness,
Yes it's fun knowing all the world has fried,
And it's fun knowing any day I'll end up
Just another one who's died.
We just love radiation
And the death of a nation –
We just love having nuclear fall-out.

Here we are, we're OK like they told us,
But the world's in a bit of a mess;
If you're wondering where we are living,
We are not, so I 'spect you can guess.

*(Each pulls a string and mechanical wings appear.)*

But it's fun being up here with the angels,
It was fun standing hours in the queue,
And it's fun knowing that if you don't change
    things
You'll be coming up here too.
We just love watching, crying
While you're all down there dying –
We just love having nuclear fall-out.

We just love nuclear fission and our great
  politicians
We just love jolly notions of some nuclear
  explosions
We just love radiation and the death of a nation
We just love having nuclear fall-out.

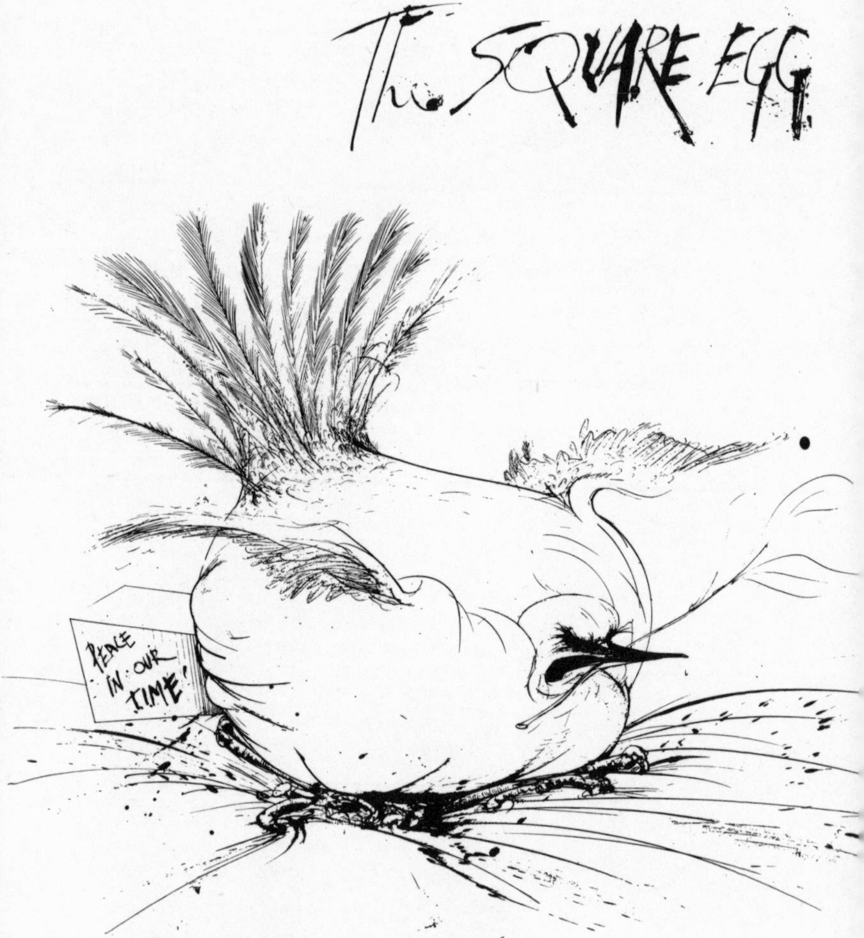
THE SQUARE EGG
PEACE IN OUR TIME
Ralph STEADman

# *Picking Sides*
ALAN BLEASDALE

**Alan:** I'm not going to take up much of your time,
which is just as well because there's not a lot of
laughs in this, and I'm certainly not going to try
and tell you how to live your lives. Why should I
insult you?

However, having said that, someone was telling
me recently about a psychoanalyst called Wilfred
'Bion' who was renowned for his study of people's
behaviour in organised groups and the behaviour
of their . . . leaders.

Now, one of his conclusions was as follows: that
if you get any group of people in a room and *ask*
for a leader to come forward, the first person to
put him or herself forward as a leader will *always*
be a paranoid schizophrenic. If such a person is not
in the room, a malignant hysteric will try to
become the leader. If a malignant hysteric is not
available because she's spending the weekend at
Chequers, a psychopathic personality with delin-
quent tendencies will offer his or her services.

So much for leaders. But what about you and
me? Well, I haven't got a clue about you, but, as
for me, I suppose I've always believed that statement that the only truly happy human being can
only be criminal, ignorant or insane.

I certainly find happiness further away now than
I ever did. For I was brought up on a diet of hope
and peace and freedom, and the possibility of a
future worth looking forward to. I am one of those
fortunate people born immediately after the
Second World War, who grew up cocooned within

the Welfare State, the influence of the 1944 Education Act, the promises of Macmillan, and the liberal pleasures of what were called, in all seriousness, 'The Swinging Sixties'.

I regret to say that, at the time unaware and young, and of course, never having had it so good – thank you, Harold – I believed that I need not contribute to the society that contributed to me. I thought someone else could do it for me.

I wasn't insane, and I'm certainly not going to tell you if I have ever been criminal, but I was ignorant. And the biggest ignorance of all was the idea I shared with millions of others – that our side would win.

The side, that is, that I would have been on if I hadn't been so ignorant and lazy and busy having fun, thinking I had found true happiness. The side of humanity, equality and liberty. The only side, surely, that *nice* people would want to be on. Because the mob we were facing represented the dark stain and the scowl on the face of human kind – the forces of prejudice, violence and bigotry, the casual wastage and carnage and cruelty that have made this century statistically and incomparably the most violent century ever known. Just past the barricades and across the corridors of power were people with position and privilege and offensive weapons and articles of torture; those for whom 'Happiness Is A Warm Gun' and 'conscience' is a dirty word. . . . And our side thought that our side would win. Because we were nice people.

And, so, fifteen years ago, many of my generation filled the streets of the capitals of the Western World and howled down a filthy little war in South East Asia. And eventually the Yanks did go home, and the Russians and the Chinese pretended they had never been there in the first place. . . . But they all went somewhere else, didn't they? They didn't really go home. Not unless home was Chile or Afghanistan, Eastern Europe or the Middle East, or now El Salvador and Nicaragua.

However, the quiet sadness of it all is that, as far as I can see, that time, all those years ago, was the last time that any of us could claim that the governments that are supposed to represent the people actually listened with half an ear to what we, the people, had to say.

These are the worst times I have ever known. I can hardly bear to read a sensible newspaper. Many of my generation, now approaching early middle age, must share that belief. And those who were once involved, who, unlike myself, carried banners and marched for peace and their beliefs, must be aware that their dreams have turned into nightmares. *But* if we continue to sit back, stunned and dulled by dreams that turned dull themselves, if we do what I did for so many years, and turn a blind eye, then I fear for the future. And all I can say in conclusion is that *now* is the time, before time runs out. It was easy then. We were kidded into thinking we were winning then. While behind our backs. . . .

You know, I have never wanted position or power. I've seen what position and power can do to good people, never mind the mad and the bad, and Kenny Everett. I think a lot of people feel like me, but sometimes in the months of melancholy that I sometimes suffer, I do begin to wonder. After all, if *we* don't want the power, look where it ends up. . . .

I leave the final words to Lenny Bruce, a so-called sick man. But this is what he said: 'My concept? You can't do anything with anybody's body to make it dirty to me. Six people, eight people, one person – the only things you can do to make it dirty are to hurt it and kill it. Hiroshima was dirty.'

# *Music*

# *Peace in Our Time*

Out of the ae ro plane stepped Chamberlain with a con-demned man's
man go - ing round ta - king names, No mat-ter who you claim to
light - ing a bon - fire up - on ev - 'ry hill - top in the

stare
be.                                                                      But
land.                                                                    As
                                                                        Just an-

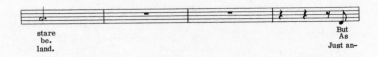

we all cheered wild - ly,   a pho-to-graph was ta - ken, as he
in - no - cent as ba - bies, A mad dog with ra - bies, you're
other tiny island in - va - ded, When he's got the

waved a piece of pa - per in the air.
still a part of some con - spi - ra - cy.
whole world in his hands.

Now the dis - co ma - chine lives in
Mean - while there's a light over the
And the heav - y - weight cham - pion fights

Mu - nich And we are all friends
o - cean, Burning brighter than the sun.
in the inter - national pro - pa - ganda star wars.

# *Ban the Bomb*

(n.c.) (Freely)

Wrap your-self in silver pa-per   Put a sand-bag on your head

Crawl in-side your fall-out shel-ter   Un-der-neath your gar-den shed.

Boil an egg   Or have a cud-dle   Cut your toe-nails   Make the bed,

By the time this re-cord's fi-nished   Ev-ery-bo-dy will be

1. Wrap your-

(sim.)

self   in sil-ver pa-per   Put a sand-bag   on your head

½ VERSE 2:   Wash your smalls feed the cactus telephone your Uncle Fred
             By the time this record's finished everybody will be dead

CHORUS      (Repeat)

# *Nuclear Fall-out*

great po-li-ti-cians. We just love having nu-cle-ar fall - out So we
fate they're de-ba-ting, We just love having nu-cle-ar fall - out. So we

bought loads of food and some wa-ter___ And we sandbagged the walls like they
were just us three in this shel-ter___ We were hav-ing a won-der-ful

said, Then we sat -neath the stairs like they told us___ They were
day; I was sick, so was I, I was burn-ing___ But we

right we're O K we're not dead, 'Cos it's fun sit-ting in here al-to-
thought what the hell a-ny-way 'Cos it's fun hav-ing ra-di-a-tion

-gether___ Yes it's fun knowing we will all get through, And it's
sickness___ Yes it's fun knowing all the world has fried, And it's

fun that the gen-'rals have as - sured us___ Ev-'ry-
fun know-ing a-ny day I'll end up___ As a-

-thing they say is true we just love jol-ly notions of some
-no-ther one who's died, We just love ra-di-a-tion and the

nu-clear ex-plosions We just love hav-ing nu-cle-ar fall out. There we
death of a na-tion We just love hav-ing nu-cle-ar fall out, Here we

are we're O K   like they told us____   But the world's in a bit   of a

mess;   If you're won - der-ing where we are li - ving____   We are

not  so I 'spect  you can  guess.   But it's  fun   be-ing up here with the

an - gels____   It was   fun stand-ing hours  in the  queue,   And it's

fun  knowing that if you don't change things____  You'll be  com - ing  up  here

too.   We  just   love watching crying While you're all down there dying, We just

love hav-ing nu - cle-ar  fall   out.  We just  love  nu-clear fission And our

great po - li-ticians We just love  jol-ly notions of some nu-clear ex-plosions We just

love ra-di-a-tion And the death of a nation We just love having nu-clear  fall  -  out.

© 1983 Alan Bence